FOREWORD BY LAJA IBRAHEEM, MD

ROYALTY

THE PROPHECY. THE PROCESS. THE PROMISE.

EMMANUEL I. CHUKWUDI

Royalty
Written By: Emmanuel I. Chukwudi

Book Completion Services Provided by:
TRU Statement Publications www.trustatementpublications.com

TRU Statement
PUBLICATIONS
www.trustatementpublications.com

Truth. Reflection. Unity.

Unless otherwise stated, all bible quotes have been taken from the King James Version (KJV)

Copyright © 2020 Emmanuel I. Chukwudi
First Printing: 2020,
Printed in the United States of America
10282020
ISBN-13: 978-1-948085-42-7

DEDICATION

To my late father, Clement Chukwudi, thank you for showing me what a real man does for his wife and children. You provided vision and direction for your household.

And to the Nigerian youths massacred at Lekki Tollgate Lagos by Nigerian armed forces, as they were peacefully protesting against corrupt leadership in the nation on October 20th, 2020. We will never forget your sacrifice and courage.

CONTENTS

FOREWORD

I was thrilled when Emmanuel asked me to write the foreword to this book. I have known Emmanuel for many years. The first time I met him was in my local church on a Sunday morning, when he would humbly ride his bicycle to attend morning services. I was attracted to him for many reasons. First, his humility, his boldness, his perseverance and his love for Christ.

His humility to ride a bicycle to a gathering in an African church where everybody comes with all kinds of luxury cars to showcase their American dream-come-true was quite impressive. He was not bothered by that; Rather, he would come in his bicycle. Nothing could stop him from coming to worship his Father!

"For who hath despised the day of small things? for they shall rejoice, and shall see the plummet in the hand of Zerubbabel with those seven; they are the eyes of the Lord, which run to and fro through the whole earth."

I have observed him seek the face of God and serve Him despite all the obstacles facing a new immigrant to the western world. He didn't allow the cares of this world and the deceitfulness of riches to distract him. I have seen over the years, his quest to serve Christ despite all odds, and his quest for knowledge and passion for the work of ministry.

I was also attracted to him because unknown to him, he reminded me of myself when I was in high school. I would proudly ride my bicycle to school daily when my friends and especially my girlfriend (presently my wife) were being driven to school in chauffeured luxury cars.

He considers me his mentor but unknown to him, I've learned more from him than I think he learned from me. I'm a passionate follower of his regular broadcasts on Facebook, YouTube and Instagram. I have also read his previous books. I cannot underestimate the gift of God and the anointing on his life.

This book is an invitation to understand who you are in God and how God sees you as His child. The scripture that comes to mind is 1 Peter 2:9:

"But ye are a chosen generation, a royal priesthood, an holy nation, a peculiar people; that ye should shew forth the praises of him who hath called you out of darkness into his marvellous light."

This book will give you a great insight into what it means to be chosen of God. It will help you to appreciate and appropriate the gifts that have been deposited in you. The author has used the lives and experiences of certain godly characters in the Bible like Esther, Joseph, Nehemiah, and Daniel to pass across his message.

I encourage anyone who wants a deeper relationship with God and who wants to proclaim His excellencies to start reading this book today.

LAJA IBRAHEEM, MD

Fellow American College of Psychiatry and Neurology.
Minister in charge Life Group Ministry,
Intl Christian Center Los Angeles

INTRODUCTION

"And they sung a new song, saying, Thou art worthy to take the book, and to open the seals thereof: for thou wast slain, and hast redeemed us to God by thy blood out of every kindred, and tongue, and people, and nation; And hast made us unto our God kings and priests: and we shall reign on the earth." – Rev 5:9-10 KJV

God has great plans for your life and as a loving father, everything about Him is good. God is good. His thoughts and plans for your life are awesome and beautiful. The blueprints of your life are simply glorious.

Because of the weight of His blessing on your life, God also sets a system in place to prepare you for your destiny. He doesn't want you to miss the great agenda He designed for your life. With this in mind, He lovingly and intentionally places certain things in place to guide you along the path through greatness. God's desire is to ultimately bring you to and connect you with your divine purpose in life.

The purpose of this book is to equip you for the amazing future God has for you. You were created to overstep and achieve uncommon feats in your generation. Your presence matters as much as your voice is needed. Your presence on earth is strategic in God's agenda. This book will show you how to position yourself to discover your destiny so that you can make a difference in your generation.

Success in life is more of a journey than a destination and God may not show you the entire picture while you are going through the process. This process is a prerequisite for the promise. It is an inevitable route through which all must go through to reach their divine promise. In every truth, the process may be painful but it is equally gainful. Be reassured that your end will be filled with joy.

I have made a study of some individuals in the scripture who went through challenging processes before they were ushered into their royal destiny. The promise is worth waiting for. The crown comes with a cross. Greatness comes with so many demands. It costs to stand out in life.

"That ye be not slothful, but followers of them who through faith and patience inherit the promises." – Hebrew 6:12KJV

Joseph had a vision of royalty but he had to experience the dry pit in a desert, the trap set by Potiphar's wife and years of incarceration before he witnessed the reality of his vision as it came to pass. Esther was destined to be the queen but she had to face the cruelty of Haman and his wicked plot before she embraced her royalty. Daniel was a man operating with uncommon wisdom but he spent a night in a lion's den. Ruth turned her back on her own people in order to go with her mother-law. She was probably mocked by people as they saw her serving Naomi and volunteering to work in the field of Boaz. She was chosen to play a part in the lineage of King David and Jesus Christ.

Jesus had to wear the crown of thorns before He could wear the crown of glory. His prayers in the garden of Gethsemane were symbolic of His death on the cross. He died in the garden right before His body got hung on the cross. His mission on earth was concluded in that moment of total surrender to God. The weight of our sins, sicknesses and sorrows rested on Him as He wept in deep agony with sweat like drops of blood dribbling down His body. Heaven remained silent and so was hell. Angels observed as that was a moment in time which was to define eternity. Jesus had an option to choose between His willingness to yield to God's will or to walk away from His final mission on earth. The devil watched with great anticipation. God also observed to see His final decision. He had the power to walk away without losing His sonship before God. But in spite of all these, He chose to lay down His own life and the fate of the whole world was connected to that moment. It was mandatory that he drank from the cup to fulfill His ultimate assignment and mandate. Jesus yielded and He carried our chastisement. He wore the crown of groaning so we could wear the crown of glory. He is the promise of the Father. The glory that was lost in the garden of Eden was restored in the garden of Gethsemane. There's a blessing connected to the pains you are going through. Your tears are not wasted.

The promises predestined for your life comes with a price. The process you are presently going through is the price to pay to realize your purpose in life. The process is not there to destroy you but to purge your intentions and desires. You are in a controlled environment. And you will emerge as pure as gold!

"Consider it a sheer gift, friends, when tests and challenges come at you from all sides. You know that under pressure, your faith-life is forced into the open and shows its true colors. So don't try to get out of anything prematurely.

*Let it do its work so you become mature and well-developed,
not deficient in any way."*

– James 1:2-4

CHAPTER ONE

JOSEPH: THE DREAMER

"Your destination is foreshadowed by your imagination."

Vision is the symbol of greatness; it captures the future in present times. Joseph was a man who had remarkable experiences of anointed dreams. Amazingly, he saw the future he could not interpret in the present. You may not capture the clarity of what God is showing you at the moment but capture the vision, document what you see and stay consistent. It is imperative to understand that visions and revelations are progressive, they come in phases. God reveals Himself to us in fragments. Dreams draw you closer to God's heart. This is emphasized in the book of *Habakkuk 2: 1-4:*

"I will stand on my guard post and station myself on the rampart; And I will keep watch to see what He will speak to me, And how I may reply when I am reproved. Then the LORD answered me and said, "Record the vision And inscribe it on tablets, That the one who reads it may run. "For the vision is yet for the appointed time; It hastens toward the goal and it will not fail. Though it tarries, wait for it; For it will certainly come, it will not delay. Behold, as for the proud one, His soul is not right within him; But the righteous will live by his faith."

Dreaming

Joseph had a dream that was bigger than his environment. He saw the sun, the moon and stars bowing down to him. Joseph's father and brothers knew the meaning of his dream, as a result, felt intimidated by it. Sometimes people see potentials that God has deposited in you even before you do.

Joseph shared his dreams with his family but they weren't comfortable with it. Not everyone that claims to love you is in love with your dreams. People want you to remain ordinary, such that the moment you tap into a higher version of yourself they become irritated. They become uncomfortable with you the moment you begin to envision yourself in a great light. This discomfort is born from an ill will to have you remain mediocre. They don't want you to leave the block and reach out to the world. They may be members of your family, school mates, church folks, coworkers or friends. It is not advisable to reveal your vision to people in a hurry. Write the vision but hide it from dream killers. The Bible in the book of *Genesis 37:18-20 says:*

"Now when they saw him afar off, even before he came near them, they conspired against him to kill him. (19) Then they said to one another, "Look, this dreamer is coming! (20) Come therefore, let us now kill him and cast him into some pit; and we shall say, 'Some wild beast has devoured him.' We shall see what will become of his dreams!"

Be careful how you share the divine ideas God placed in your heart. Protect your dreams. The enemy sees the potentials deposited in you. Pharaoh saw the future of Moses as a little child and ordered the killing of all children of his age. King Herod ordered the killing of children when Jesus was born. He saw His glory even when He was still an infant. Your vision is a threat to someone close to you. Shield your ideas and plans.

Lost in the Desert

Jacob sent Joseph to go visit his brothers in the field and take lunch to them. But he got lost in the desert. He was humble enough to seek the guidance of a stranger. God positioned a destiny helper to point him in the right path. He was willing to ask questions. You need the experience of those who have gone ahead of you in life. In the multitude of counsel there is safety. Someone has been positioned strategically to guide you through the path of life, so ask questions. Don't assume you know the way. You need destiny helpers in your life's journey. You inevitably need divine direction to stay on the path of your vision and get to your destination.

Every mistake made in life is a consequence of the absence of guidance. Human guidance may be dangerous. Elisha engaged Prophet Elijah in a conversation before Elijah was taken from him. He caught the mantle but he also received mentorship. The prodigal son received his share of the father's wealth but he missed the necessary training required to secure it. It takes humility to sustain inheritance. Solomon endured as the wisest and wealthiest king that ever lived because he listened to the counsel of his father David. He sat at the feet of his father to receive the words of wisdom. Having a gift cannot supersede the need for godly wisdom. Ruth needed Naomi's guidance to locate the field of Boaz. A mentor is one assigned to help you navigate through the uncertainties of life.

The Stolen Coat

The brothers of Joseph saw him coming from afar and plotted against him. They targeted the coat of many colors placed on him by his father, a symbol of his royal destiny. God loves colors; He designed the garment of the high priest with different colors. God used the rainbow to enact a covenant with man after the flood in Noah's time.

The brothers of Joseph tore his garment, but they couldn't tear apart his destiny because his greatness was deposited in his spirit. Greatness always lies within. The garment of Jesus was torn off from his body but His royalty was untouched. The devil always goes for the superficial but God knows how to frustrate the plans of the devil to protect one's future. They can take your garment but they cannot touch your mantle. God hides your future inside you. The garment just serves as a symbol.

The enemy killed the body of Jesus and buried it, not recognizing he was hastening the fulfilment of God's divine agenda for our redemption. Those fighting you are simply helping to tilt you towards God's ultimate plan for your life. The Bible reveals that the devil wished he never killed the king

4

of glory. Every attack waged against your life makes you stronger, wiser and more glorious. The present challenge in your life is a divine set up for your star to rise. God cannot be taken by surprise. Your steps are perfectly orchestrated and ordered by God to usher you into destiny. Everything is working out for your own good and you shall surely fulfil destiny.

The enemy believed that by afflicting the body of Job, his greatness would be terminated; but God hid the glory of Job in his spirit. The Bible says, *"The spirit of man is the candle of the Lord"*. The devil couldn't touch Job's greatness. Job emerged a better man after his trials. He went through fire and came out as gold. Gold is a great treasure. You are coming out refined and renewed. God can use your enemies to push you forward in life.

'You prepare a table or banquet for me right in the face of my haters.'

– Psalm 23:5

God can Use Anyone to Bless You

Joseph was thrown into a dry well as suggested by Reuben. Judah further advised that they trade him as a slave. The Ishmaelites were used as vehicles to convey Joseph into his great future. They thought he was doomed but unknown to them was the fact that they were instrumental to the fulfilment of God's plans in his life. His brothers rejoiced and were feasting when he was bundled up and sold as a slave. They were used by God to thrust Joseph a little further towards his dream. It was a divine strategy, set up to bring him closer to the fulfilment of his destiny. They sold him just like Jesus.

The dream may take time before it is brought into manifestation. The vision may put you through the dry pit, but be encouraged because you are being strategically linked to the place God designed for you in life. You may find yourself in an unpleasant situation at this moment. Your present situation may not look like the dream God revealed to you, however, it is pertinent you remain consistent. You are being processed for a better future which is a conspiracy for your glorification in life. Preparation may take time but manifestation comes overnight.

Jacob wept over the feigned death of Joseph after his sons brought back Joseph's blood-stained garment to him. His sons lied to him about the death of Joseph and said that a beast devoured Joseph. But God always plans ahead of the enemy. Your royal destiny is a sealed agenda in the mind of God which will be brought to manifestation at the right time. Your life is a book already written by God before your birth. This book was delivered to your angel who watches over you to ensure you fulfill everything written in that book. Your steps are divinely ordered!

"Then said I, Lo, I come: in the volume of the book it is written of me."

– Psalm 40:7

You are under a divine watch and monitor. You won't miss destiny. Even your mistakes in life can't cancel God's ordained plan for your life. Glorious things are spoken of you in the volume of the book. Your times on earth are in God's hands. Don't be afraid. The affliction is a tool in the hands of God to bring you further into your promised destiny. Your promise is untouchable by the enemy.

Royal Trap

Joseph lived a consecrated life before God. He vowed to please God even as a slave in Egypt. He became a steward in the house of Potiphar. His master's wife was interested in him. She also saw the seed of greatness in him. The enemy knows what you carry. Delilah knew what Samson was carrying in him. The anointing attracts predators. Greatness has an attractive aura. And the enemy sets uncommon traps for uncommon people. He could sense when God's hand is upon a man. The enemy has a strategy for the fall of every great man. You cannot be ignorant of his devices. Be conscious of what you carry.

Joseph turned down the ungodly request of his master's wife. He was not enticed by her position, beauty or promises. God already gave him a greater promise. His love for God couldn't let him defile himself. He feared God. Heaven and hell observed tenaciously that defining moment. He pleased God and heaven took record of that moment. He kept his own part of the covenant. Whenever the enemy presents you with an enticing gift, heaven turns its gaze at you to see your reaction.

Take a stand for God. You are the hope of your generation. Preserve the covenant!

Potiphar's wife lied against Joseph and he was thrown into the prison. But he was still faithful in the prison. Joseph saw that as another opportunity to develop himself. He kept upgrading his leadership skills by serving other prisoners. True leaders serve their people; and every storm or challenge before them is an opportunity for growth.

> *Genesis 39:21-23 " But the Lord was with Joseph, and shewed him mercy, and gave him favor in the sight of the keeper of the prison. And the keeper of the prison committed to Joseph's hand all the prisoners that were in the prison; and whatsoever they did there, he was the doer of it. The keeper of the prison looked not to anything that was under his hand; because the Lord was with him, and that which he did, the Lord made it to prosper. "*

Excellence Cannot be Hidden

An excellent spirit speaks everywhere. The good qualities of Joseph were not hidden even in the dark seasons of his life. His challenging moments were his training moments. His faith in the infallible word of God kept him hopeful. God's favor followed him to the prison because his heart was clean. The supervisor in the jail saw the hand of God on his life and handed his own assignment over to him. Joseph didn't take that for granted. Favor is not to be wasted; it is given by God for service. He took advantage of that rare privilege to prepare himself. His role in prison became a training ground for the big picture.

The sun, moon and stars bowed down to him in his dream; nevertheless, he needed to train himself to grow into the dream he saw. The process prunes us. God will never put you in a position you have not prepared for. It's not enough to see it in your spirit; you must get trained for it. Depth determines height. The purpose of the process is to shape you for the purpose of your life. Joseph saw beyond the walls of the prison; he saw the crown and throne of Egypt. He saw the golden ring. He saw his beautiful wife and children. He saw himself overseeing the affairs of the nation as the governor. Other prisoners saw the heavy chains around their ankles, hands and necks. Your vision is your channel out of obscurity. God gives you dreams to keep you hopeful through the process.

Apostle Paul demanded that his notes and books be sent to him while incarcerated. He wrote a greater part of his epistles while in chains. The body can be imprisoned but not the spirit. Make every moment count. God has deposited greatness in you; it's your responsibility to awaken those endowments and put them to work.

Your gift will attract haters. It will also attract favor. The complication is a part of God's divine agenda to build your faith. You are on schedule with destiny, so get ready because your time of revealing is coming.

A True Leader Solves Problems

Joseph embodied the wisdom of God from his youth. Wisdom is having a supernatural knowledge to resolve problems. He didn't lose his special gift while in prison. Discernment is profitable in challenging moments. Our God-given gifts are not for self-exaltation or glorification. We are designed and sent to be a blessing to our world. We came to serve the world with our divine endowments. Freely we've received, freely we must give.

Joseph was sensitive to the needs of people around him. His discerning attribute made him notice the burden in the hearts of the chief Baker and Butler. His leadership potential was also expressed at that moment. Leaders see problems and solve them. It takes wisdom to see a disorder in your environment. Leaders have eyes for details. A true leader shows compassion. The book of *Psalm 105:16-22* says:

Moreover, He called for a famine in the land; He destroyed all the provision of bread. He sent a man before them— Joseph—who was sold as a slave. They hurt his feet with fetters, He was laid in irons. Until the time that his word came to pass, The word of the Lord tested him. The king sent and released him, The ruler of the people let him go free. He made him lord of his house, And ruler of all his possessions, To bind his princes at his pleasure, And teach his elders wisdom.

A divine test precedes every promotion in life. This is why God must train you and test you in order to ascertain your readiness for His blessing. Joseph was sensitive to his time. He prepared himself ahead of time. God's word followed him all through his waiting period and he didn't disappoint God. He remained faithful in the face of rejection, temptation and accusation. Heaven watched in silence to observe him in strategic moments. God observed his responses to those trying times. God's silence is not a sign of rejection. The teacher remains silent during his test.

There have been times in my life when I didn't feel God's presence around me. But I have learned to trust Him. I think it's also a great proof of trust when He is silent. The bond has grown so deep now, that words are not necessary to validate His presence. Sometimes silence is a sign of trust and oneness, so be reminded that you are not alone in such moments of silence. There were great men in the Bible that experienced these silent moments; men such as Job, and even our Lord Jesus Christ. When He felt the weight of the cross while praying in the garden, He asked God to move the cup from Him. But God was silent. When Abraham was leaving his father's house to an unknown destination God was silent. When he took his only son to offer as sacrifice, God was silent. God can be silent!

The Prince of Egypt

Pharaoh had a dream that none of his wise men could interpret. Through Pharaoh's dream, God created a platform for Joseph, the slave boy to realize his vision. The chief butler finally remembered and recommended Joseph to the king. Joseph interpreted the dream by the wisdom of God. He was made the governor of Egypt and second-in-command to Pharaoh. Joseph passed the test and was released from prison; he excelled in the test by the virtue of patience. He passed the test of character by forgiving his own brothers. He also passed the test of purity by turning down the ungodly request of his master's wife. Joseph placed all his trust in God even when the chief cupbearer forgot about him. His consecration vindicated him. The gift of God in his life helped him to interpret the king's dream which brought him to royalty in Egypt. Dream again. Pass the test!

"God can make you go through what you hate, so He can give you what He loves."

-Hans Tawi

CHAPTER TWO

ESTHER: THE INTERCESSOR

"Therefore, if it pleases the king, let him issue a royal decree and let it be written in the laws of Persia and Media, which cannot be repealed, that Vashti is never again to enter the presence of King Xerxes. Also let the king give her royal position to someone else who is better than she."

— Esther 1:19

The Spirit of Jezebel

Nobody is irreplaceable in God's agenda. Lucifer lost his place in heaven. Judas lost his place to greed. Queen Vashti was rejected because of her rebellion. Nebuchadnezzar lost his throne because of pride. Saul lost his place because of his disobedience. It's important to note that someone has what it takes to replace you. So you must be diligent in handling that which God has entrusted in your care, lest you lose it.

Vision invigorates you with the zeal to press forward for the goal notwithstanding the opposition you may encounter along the way; it is stronger than the will to quit; it's a passion that is deeper than death. Vision sees the invisible and attempts the impossible. Vision is the mark of greatness. Esther was a slave girl who saw a queen in herself. She wore the garment of a housemaid with the mindset of a queen. Her state didn't stop her from seeing a future that could be accomplished. People of vision endure the challenges of life knowing that storms come to make them stronger. They look for opportunities to grow, they take up more responsibilities, and they don't quit.

Esther saw an opening in the palace for a new queen, a position that was lost by queen Vashti. Vashti didn't value her place. She didn't honor the king. She went ahead to set up her own banquet with other high-class women in the city ignoring the king's banquet. That was the spirit of pride, the spirit of Jezebel. She wanted her own platform against the king's instruction. Leaders want those that honor their instructions close to them. Honor is an access key. You attract what you honor.

The Making of Esther

Esther humbled herself before Mordecai. Mordecai mentored and groomed her. He understood royal etiquettes. She was teachable because she was willing to listen and be led. A rebellious person will surely lose his or her place in life. Humility enthrones while pride dethrones. The book of *Esther 2:20* says that:

> *"But Esther had kept secret her family background and nationality just as Mordecai had told her to do, for she continued to follow Mordecai's instructions as she had done when he was bringing her up."*

Esther was approved for her humility. She wasn't disobedient to Mordecai, her uncle. Her meekness and the favor of God upon her earned her a place in the heart of Mordecai who also prepared her for the position of the queen. Mordecai was Esther's destiny helper. God used him to train Esther for royalty; he was the bridge that gave her entrance into royalty. Don't ignore the person sent by God to train you for destiny. When you are preparing for the next phase of your life, God may plant you in a local place to prepare you for a global assignment. Great people are trained in neglected places. Sometimes, kings are born in mangers. Don't ignore the days of little beginnings. Be excellent on your level. Give your present task your best and get qualified for the next level.

I have come to understand that no experience is a waste. This was born from the fact that everything I learned from my experiences, over the years, tend to resurface at every level. God will not allow you pass through a test or trial in vain. Even the challenges we go through play a part in our story. The Holy Spirit has inspired divine ideas in crushing seasons of my life. The seeds of destiny grow out of adversity.

Where you are is a stepping stone to your next assignment. But you must pass the test in order to proceed to the next stage. The process is an inevitable route to the promise. Don't be casual with your present task; attend to it with all diligence. You are being tested for your next assignment. You are being observed by someone who has the power to recommend you for a greater position. Take responsibilities. Develop your skills. You will need the experience in your next assignment. Esther prepared herself to be a queen by carrying out her house chores effectively. Mordecai took notice of her character and integrity. You are being watched!

One Night with The King

The king chose Esther to be his wife. Her meekness opened doors for her. However, God positioned her as queen for the preservation of His people against Haman's anti-Semitic plan. Esther's presence in the palace was the system set by God to liberate His people. God had a bigger plan. The blessing on your life is not just for you and your family. God needed a channel through which He would release the blessing. He chose you for a purpose. God picked a slave girl (Esther) to be the channel through which He would preserve His people. The kingdom agenda is the big picture. God is not motivated by pleasure but by His divine purpose.

The Purpose of Favor

Haman's hatred for the Jews caused him to come up with a plan to destroy them. His hatred for Mordecai extended to the Jews. He obtained authorization from the king to carry out his wicked plan. When Haman's plan was disclosed to the Jews, they were distressed; they wept and cried out. Mordecai sent a word to Esther to go present the case to the king. Mordecai made her to understand that her mission in the palace was to intercede for God's people, and not just for her own pleasure; she was on a divine mission. Being a queen was a channel through which she would fulfill her assignment as an intercessor to deliver the

Jews. God appointed her a queen at a strategic time to protect His people and preserve their generation on earth. She took the challenge to present herself before the king against the royal order. That was a suicidal step of action. But prayers were being raised on her behalf by the Jews.

The fulfilment of your destiny will require a fight. You need to understand that great things don't just happen; you will encounter oppositions. The vision God gave you will face resistance from the devil through people, especially those close to you. This resistance is a common experience faced by those that are called to accomplish great things. It is important to note that the higher the call of God upon your life, the greater the resistance you will experience. The attack you receive from people can be a sign of approval from God. The enemy can use the people you respect to hurt you. So it's not about you; it's about the call on your life. Stay strong and be confident in the Lord. God's business won't suffer because someone attacked your reputation. Your purpose is more important than your pain or pleasure. Your greatest attack will come from those you love.

Your success at every stage of your life could be unveiled through the challenges you face and overcome. However, to overcome every challenge you face in life, you need the help of the Holy Spirit. Sometimes God would allow things wrong in our lives in order to turn our attention to Him. So, if you are held up in a situation, seek the face of the Lord. What seems to be the end of the road, only leads to the beginning of another. Brace up; be strong in the Lord. You were built for this moment. The challenge is a divine set up for your ultimate victory.

The book of *Esther 2:12* says:

" Now when every maid's turn was come to go in to king Ahasuerus, after that she had been twelve months, according to the manner of the women, (for so were the days of their purifications accomplished, to wit, six months with oil of myrrh, and six months with sweet odors, and with other things for the purifying of the women;)"

The Palace Protocol

You don't stand before royalty by chance. Destiny demands preparation because preparation places value on you. The weight of your glory is directly proportional to the depth of your training. Training periods aren't pleasant; however, your public manifestation reveals your private engagement. God knows when you are ready.

Esther had to go through the process of purification before she was fit to go before the king. Joseph received a makeover when he left the prison before he was presented to the king. Royalty will demand preparedness. Success is not cheap. There is a price tag!

Esther was a slave girl with a difference. Your nationality does not determine your place in life. It is mindset that sets a person apart from his contemporaries. Visionary people think differently. They prepare today for the promise of their tomorrow. They don't sit back and watch life ride them along. They determine their destination. So consciously equip yourself because royalty doesn't summon a mediocre.

Esther was trained and processed for her moment, to captivate the greatest man in the land, the king. A virtuous woman carries an irresistible fragrance. That was the force that pulled Boaz towards Ruth. Purity attracted Boaz. Seduction attracted Samson. Kings place virtue over beauty.

My major purpose in life is to bring people into a stronger relationship with God. I knew as a teenager that purity can take me anywhere on the surface of the earth. I made a strong covenant with God over my life to stay consecrated. That singular step earned me the favor of God that still speaks in my life. I live under a sworn oath to serve God for life. Consecration triggers favor. Esther separated herself from other ladies in town. She focused on her job and the king took notice of her. Her purity gave her an attractive aura.

There are places you cannot go in life until you enter into a covenant of consecration with God. Royalty has a price. It responds to spiritual responsibility. Sit up and build up the spiritual stamina needed for your place in life. The King is waiting. Nations are under bondage expecting your rising. Your generation is under the trap of the enemy. You are the hope and answer to your generation. Rise to the occasion. Prepare for royalty. This is your time! The Bible, in the book of *Rom 12:1-2 (Amplified version)* says:

"Therefore I urge you, brothers and sisters, by the mercies of God, to present your bodies [dedicating all of yourselves, set apart] as a living sacrifice, holy and well-pleasing to God, which is your rational (logical, intelligent) act of worship. And do not be conformed to this world [any longer with its superficial values and customs], but be transformed

and progressively changed [as you mature spiritually] by the renewing of your mind [focusing on godly values and ethical attitudes], so that you may prove [for yourselves] what the will of God is, that which is good and acceptable and perfect [in His plan and purpose for you].

Esther was preferred over other ladies because she purified herself. Boaz chose Ruth because she set herself apart from others. This is seen in the book of *Ruth 3:10:*

> *"And he said, Blessed be thou of the LORD, my daughter: for thou hast shewed more kindness in the latter end than at the beginning, inasmuch as thou followedst not young men, whether poor or rich."*

> *"Go, gather together all the Jews that are present in Shushan, and fast ye for me, and neither eat nor drink three days, night or day: I also and my maidens will fast likewise; and so will I go in unto the king, which is not according to the law: and if I perish, I perish." – Esther 4:16 KJV*

Everyone won't always believe in you. Your destiny will attract great resistance from the kingdom of darkness. This resistance will manifest itself through people, and situations. Some people are assigned to bring you down; to keep you from fulfilling God's purpose for your life. Challenges come to make you ready for what lies ahead. Greatness attracts strong attacks. Joseph, David, Daniel and Jesus Christ had to face great opposition. You will meet them at work, in church and even among your family members. They see your future and know what God has ordained for you. Their mission is to sabotage your purpose and puncture your testimony. Your future is a threat to the kingdom of hell.

The Evil Plot

Esther had gained favor before the king but Haman was not happy. He requested permission of the king to destroy the Jews. He was uncomfortable with the growth and expansion of the Jews in the land. Jews are a special kind of people. They carry the gem of Abraham and other covenant fathers. They grow, expand and take over anywhere they go. *Exodus 1:19* says:

> *"And the midwives said unto Pharaoh, Because the Hebrew women are not as the Egyptian women; for they are lively, and are delivered ere the midwives come in unto them."*

Jews don't fail, beg, quit or lose. This is because they've been chosen by God to be His people. Haman was very unsettled about the Jews. He planned to use the king's influence to terminate them.

The evil agenda of Haman brought fear and terror in the land. The Jews needed an advocate. And Mordecai sent a word to Esther, the chosen queen.

Esther 4:14 says:

"For if thou altogether holdest thy peace at this time, then shall there enlargement and deliverance arise to the Jews from another place; but thou and thy father's house shall be destroyed: and who knoweth whether thou art come to the kingdom for such a time as this?"

Esther took up the challenge and declared a fast. She was ready to risk her life to deliver her people. God sent her to stand as an intercessor at that dreadful time. She took up the challenge to represent her people. She needed to fortify herself for this risky venture so she asked her people to go on a fast for three days on her behalf.

You cannot enter into your promise unprepared. There are giants in your promise land. A wise man once said that the promised land is not a tourist center. You have to fight the giants occupying it. Preparation is a vital key to your manifestation; spiritual readiness is profound and strategic. God does not place a novice before royalty. He may anoint you but He expects you to sharpen your skills. He will not serve you raw to the world. So He spends more time working on you, incubating and putting structure in your life. His intention is to bring discipline and order in your life. People without discipline abuse the grace on their lives.

Esther was mentored by Mordecai; she was dipped in oil for several months just for a one-night encounter with the king. Nobody walks into royalty unprepared.

Success in any assignment will require sacrifice; and sacrifice when made isn't pleasant. So get used to stepping away from your comfort zone. Pay the price ahead. Slay your giants early. Read books. Stay up, sit up and stand out. Be rounded in your thought; know a bit of everything needed for your calling; be balanced, but be a genius in something organic to you. When you appear before the king, he should hold up his golden scepter. Your gift should make room for you. Assume your spot and shine. Don't be a mediocre in your calling. The world is waiting for you; and the world is yours.

God has chosen you for a great task. That is the only reason He allowed you pass through so many challenges and tests; some of which were painful. The pains you've passed through on account of those challenging situations shouldn't be in vain. Don't waste your pain. The burden you feel is divine. The weight on your shoulder shouldn't be ignored. Your sleeplessness is not insomnia; it's your dreams crying out within you and seeking for a way out. Get up, write that vision, and pursue it. Run with the vision. You are next in line.

You will cause great harm to this generation if you fail to identify and explore the gifts and divine deposits in your life. Esther identified her divine purpose as queen over the land, and she accomplished that purpose. The book of *Esther 8:1* says:

"On that day did the king Ahasuerus give the house of Haman the Jews' enemy unto Esther the queen. And Mordecai came before the king; for Esther had told what he was unto her."

Esther showed her love for her people in many ways. She didn't allow her royal position to distract her from her mission.

She retained her humility. The fate of the entire Jews was in her hands. Haman plotted to destroy the Jewish people, and he obtained the authorization from the king to execute his plans. However, God put Queen Esther in a dignified position to stand in the gap and intercede for the Jews.

God only brings you to the place of favor and blessing for the advancement of His kingdom on earth. Queen Esther used the favor she received from God to intercede for the preservation of God's people. You are blessed to be a blessing. God needs a willing vessel through which He can pour out His grace on others. He chooses selfless people to carry His mandate. It's a privilege to be chosen by God.

Esther exuded great wisdom. She understood her influence as a woman and when to apply it to situations. The power of influence is a natural gift every woman carries. Esther maximized the favor she'd received from God before the king. She was sent to the palace at a defining moment.

Hanged on His Trap

The king discovered the wicked plot of Haman. Haman had a selfish intention to destroy the Jews in the land especially Mordecai who refused to bow to him. The king gave an order for Haman to be hanged on the same gallows he prepared for Mordecai; and Jews were not destroyed. Don't underestimate the power of a praying woman. The greatest weapon of every woman is not her mouth but her knees. You win your wars on your knees. Set up a prayer altar and begin to intercede for your household. Raise war against the kingdom of darkness that is after your marriage. Daughter of Zion, this is not the time to chase after mundane things. It's time to fight the invisible enemy sent to devour the peace in your home. You are the intercessor; stand up and cry out to God. The devil dreads the voice of a praying woman. I am where I am today because of the prayers of my mother. She didn't let the devil have me.

Women have such tremendous force in the spirit realm when they pray. Don't sit back and watch the devil destroy your home and tear down all you have labored for all these years. Be the intercessor and cry out to God. Stand in the gap. Build up the hedge and hold up the hands of your man in prayers. You are his helper and not his rival. Complement him, don't compete with him. Hold up the pillars of your family from your secret place. Help him build his vision. Support him in fulfilling his calling and assignment in life. Be his backbone and secret armor. Don't be like Queen Vashti; be like Queen Esther. Never let third parties turn you against your household. There are demonic agents sent out to divide marriages. Your marriage is worth fighting for; your home is worth protecting. You are called to help your king fulfill his destiny. *Proverbs 31:29* says:

> *"Many women have done wonderful things, but you've outclassed them all."*

Favor comes with a price. In fact, favor places a huge responsibility on you. Esther found favor before the king, and she used the opportunity to intercede on behalf of the Jews. She brought freedom by risking her own life for the Jews. God brings us to success so we can use the platform to better the lives of others.

When you desire to be a blessing to people's lives, God will continue to promote you. God placed Esther in the palace because of her heart for the people of God. She had a part to play in God's plan for His people. God positioned Mordecai in the kingdom too because he desired to fight for the Jews. You have no business engaging in anything that does not advance the lives of others around you.

Sweet Slaughter

The king had granted Esther her wish. The favor of God is for a reason. God's favor broke all protocols. A slave girl became the queen of the land. Esther didn't leave any stone unturned in her quest to free the Jews from the evil plots of Haman and his household. Mordecai was rewarded for his selfless service and kindness to the king, while Haman was hanged on the gallows he prepared for Mordecai. The Jews destroyed their enemies. They fought with their own swords and brought down their foes. The Israelites had to fight to possess the land. Every open door comes with a fight. Favor will put you to work. Freedom is not free; it comes with responsibility. Never ask God for favor if you are unwilling to fight! Never ask God for favor if you are selfish! Favor is for service to mankind. You have found favor; now use it to set others free!

"Everything God gives you is for the advancement of His kingdom on earth."

CHAPTER THREE

DANIEL: THE SEER

"But Daniel purposed in his heart that he would not defile himself with the portion of the king's meat, nor with the wine which he drank: therefore he requested of the prince of the eunuchs that he might not defile himself." – Daniel 1:8

Excellence is not cheap. It takes discipline, hard work and consistent devotion to your assignment. Uncommon men and women stand out from their peers by their determined decision to pursue a greater calling. That was the case of Daniel in a strange land. He was among the young men chosen by the king to be trained for royal stewardship. The king determined the food and drinks they would take in preparation for this task.

Oath of Consecration

Daniel had a great vision for the kingdom. He wanted to be a solution to a problem. He saw a greater future beyond the position of a royal steward. He saw himself as one who would be used by God to bring solutions to problems; he saw himself as one who would be put in a dignified position to determine the fate of the nation. He saw himself counseling generations of kings in the land. Daniel made himself a demand by setting a high standard of integrity.

The call on your life will place a heavy responsibility on you; and setting a higher goal for excellence gives you the zeal needed to pursue your vision without distraction. Focus brings speed and energy.

Excellence demands diligence. God does not place kingdom treasures in the hands of a casual person. Common people produce common results while uncommon people produce uncommon results.

Daniel was a man on another level. As a slave in a foreign land he set the pace and blazed the trail for others to follow his lead. He was described as a god with the wisdom of angels because of his supernatural lifestyle. His submission to God produced a giant out of him.

Responsibility is the bread of great minds. They don't sit around to see things happen; they push further to see it come to pass. The goal you have set will place a heavy demand on your shoulder. You will be awake when others are asleep to think, pray and plan. If you want to take the lead in your field, your life will be different from others in so many ways. You will have to set higher standards for them in many areas. They are looking up to you to set the pace. You will not disappoint your generation.

There are moments that God would put you in a position to be the light. You will have to muster the courage to take fearless steps for others to follow. You shape the thoughts of people by influencing their decisions. God trusts you to shape the future; that is why He sent you to this generation in such a critical time. You are equipped to heal the land.

Chosen

Daniel stepped out and went even further in his consecration because he has the spirit of a leader. Leadership is a spirit. The other three Hebrew boys looked up to him. His passion for purity was strong. Like Daniel, God has raised you to represent Him in a dark world. Take the baton and run your race. Generations are awaiting your victory. Be the answer to the prayers of others. Daniel lived a blameless life, such that his adversaries found no fault in his actions. The book of *Daniel 6:5* says:

"Then these men said, "We shall not find any charge against this Daniel unless we find it against him concerning the law of his God."

There are forces sent to terminate God's plans for your life. Your glorious future is a threat to the devil. He has vowed to fight and keep you from realizing your destiny. The enemy always attacks you in your area of calling. But be encouraged because God watches over those who put their trust in Him. You will emerge a different person.

Conspiracy

Daniel was a faithful servant. The king loved him and placed him above other leaders in the land. This act of favor made other governors jealous. They plotted against Daniel to set him up. But God saw their evil plan.

A law was passed in the land that everyone must worship the god instituted by the king. This they did and convinced the king to put his royal seal on it as an irrevocable order. Their target was to destroy Daniel's reputation before the king. His integrity had won him the heart of the king above everyone else. They were jealous of him.

Love in the Lions' Den

Daniel ignored the king's decree and went home to pray to His God with his windows open towards Jerusalem. The fear of the Lord in him made him disregard the consequence of his action. Subsequently, he got arrested and put in the lions' den to be devoured by the beasts as a penalty for disregarding royal decree. But God sent an angel to shut the mouths of the lions and keep them from hurting him. Daniel fellowshipped in the lions' den; he came out of the lion's den unharmed. The king loved Daniel because of his faithfulness, diligence and most importantly, the favor of God. Daniel's accusers were given the punishment that was imposed on Daniel; they and their households were put in the lions' den and the lions devoured them all.

Let God fight for you while you hold your peace. Every anointed person in the Bible faced fiery attacks from enemies. Jesus was hated. Joseph was hated and sold out by his own brothers. Jabez was cursed by his own mother. David was rejected by his own father. Job was greatly afflicted by the devil. All these men had a more glorious ending than their beginning.

The path to success is filled with distractions. Focus on your assignment. Ignore the critics. Strive to please God alone. The journey may not make sense but your destination is already established. Your end will be greater than the beginning.

Consecration is a place of separation from the world to God. You cannot bond with God until you separate yourself from the world. The Bible says that friendship with the world is enmity with God. God has called every Christian to live a consecrated lifestyle. God is Holy and He demands that His children are holy just as He is. Every great man in the Bible lived a consecrated life before God. The system of the world should not shape your thoughts. You should set the pace for others to follow. You are light to the world, a world that is engrossed in thick darkness. God wants you to shine your light that the whole world would see and give Him the glory. He wants to use your life as a channel through which men will glorify His name. He is counting on you to make the difference by setting the pace.

Consecration makes you one with God. You become transformed into a divine being by living like Christ. Others look onto you to model the life of heaven for them. You become a living epistle. This was the life Daniel lived in his days. The Bible says that he refused to eat the king's meal. He separated himself to seek God. He separated himself from the system. This Hebrew boy refused to go with popular ideas. He carved out a different path to please God.

Daniel was not out to please the king. He was not afraid to reject the king's offer. Because he feared and honored God, God gave him such favor before the eyes of the king, to a point that he was like a god to the king. Consecration makes you a fearful force before the world. That was the life of Moses. The Bible says that Moses became a god unto Pharaoh. His mere footsteps in the palace made the king tremble with fear. Consecration will put you in the very class of God. You would become a terror to what used to terrify you.

Sin destroys glory. The sin of David stopped him from building the temple for God, his greatest dream in life. The sin of Samson destroyed his vision. He didn't fulfill his glorious destiny. The sin of Solomon made him lose part of his kingdom. Don't give yourself reasons to live in sin. Give yourself reasons to live a disciplined life. You are God's oracle.

"Then was the secret revealed unto Daniel in a night vision. Then Daniel blessed the God of heaven." – Daniel 2:19.

There is a price for value. You have to put in the required work to get the desired result. Daniel was chosen from among his peers because he separated himself to pay the needed price. He went the extra mile in his assignment.

The Queen Mother Testifies

The king had a dream which nobody could interpret. He was troubled and threatened to kill all his magicians. But Daniel took up the challenge to go seek the face of God, to restore the dream and also get the interpretation. The dream was revealed to him in the secret place.

Daniel had a strong relationship with God that equipped him to handle complicated situations. His daily devotion and godly lifestyle were structures that built him up to face challenges. You don't prepare in the battlefield. You don't train in the ring of a championship match. Great stars in any field pay their price early before any demand is placed on their skills.

Preparation time is very essential. It is in such periods that the courage to carry the weight of your assignment is formed. Capacity comes with practice so put your skills to work daily. Daniel was a man focused on his mission. The king bowed down and worshipped him because of the level of insight that was bestowed upon him. He was smarter than his peers. The queen described him as an angel of light. God gave Daniel divine revelation.

But he worked on himself to get there. He was a reader. The Bible says that he understood by the books. That was why he stood out from his peers. He was a man given to prayer and fasting. That was why he commanded the supernatural. There is always what to do to attain God's set target for your life. Great things happen to those that prepare ahead of time. You have an enviable destiny but you must pay the necessary price to get there.

The bible says in *Daniel 5:11-12:*

"There is a man in thy kingdom, in whom is the spirit of the holy gods; and in the days of thy father light and understanding and wisdom, like the wisdom of the gods, was found in him; whom the king Nebuchadnezzar thy father, the king, I say, thy father, made master of the magicians, astrologers, Chaldeans, and soothsayers; Forasmuch as an excellent spirit, and knowledge, and understanding, interpreting of dreams, and shewing of hard sentences, and dissolving of doubts, were found in the same Daniel, whom the king named Belteshazzar: now let Daniel be called, and he will shew the interpretation."

Daniel was a man of unusual wisdom and insight. The king needed someone to interpret the handwriting on the wall and none of his magicians could do so. God frowned at the king because he defiled the sacred vessels by using them to dine at his party with his wives and concubines. They were praising the gods of gold. God was furious with him and wrote a mysterious message on the wall of his palace. This left the king in fear and desperation. The writing was mysterious to the natural mind.

The queen recommended Daniel to be called upon for the interpretation of the strange writing on the wall. She knew Daniel's unmatchable wisdom in the land from the days of Nebuchadnezzar. The king invited Daniel and sought for his divine insight to unravel the writing on the wall.

Daniel interpreted the message sent from God to the king. Discretion is divine knowing. It is the God order of insight on a matter. Godly wisdom is stronger than human intelligence.

Godly wisdom operates heaven's perspective on earthly matters.

Daniel had an uncommon dimension of light. Through Godly wisdom, he was made outstanding among his peers; he had an excellent spirit within him. He was a man that spent time with God. Secrets are only revealed in the secret place. Every man and woman that will make a mark in this generation must learn how to maximize the secret place. It's in the place of prayer that heaven meets earth. The book of *Daniel 6:1-3* says:

> *"It pleased Darius to set over the kingdom an hundred and twenty princes, which should be over the whole kingdom;*
>
> *² And over these three presidents; of whom Daniel was first: that the princes might give accounts unto them, and the king should have no damage.*
>
> *³ Then this Daniel was preferred above the presidents and princes, because an excellent spirit was in him; and the king thought to set him over the whole realm."*

The queen was right. She had so much faith and trust in the God of Daniel. The spirit of excellence, light, understanding and divine concepts were found in Daniel.

A god Among Men

The king was humbled by the depth of Daniel's wisdom. Daniel interpreted the mystery without demanding for any reward. He accorded the glory to God who gave him the divine interpretation. Daniel acknowledged the fact that interpretation of dreams and mysteries come from God; He didn't want to take the place of God before the people. He returned glory to God. Humility is the true sign of greatness.

The king exalted Daniel over other magicians, astrologers, Chaldeans and governors. Daniel was put in charge of the kingdom like Joseph. These slaves became royal forces in a strange land by their integrity before the Lord; by their decision to honor the Lord against all odds.

God rewards faithfulness. He sees your heart and knows when you are genuinely serving Him. He is committed to blessing you as you stay fully committed to the work committed into your hands. You are called to serve. The spirit of stewardship is the right mindset. However, your motive for stewardship is very vital. Stewardship should be to God and not for man's cheap appraisal. No man can pay you; God pays the best. He pays the most and His pay is unmatchable. Stay responsible in your assignment.

"The secret of the LORD is with those who fear Him,
And He will show them His covenant."

CHAPTER FOUR

NEHEMIAH: THE BUILDER

"It takes courage to build."

The Heart of an Intercessor

Every intercessor possesses the spirit of compassion, a deep burden for the souls of men. An intercessor stands in the gap for the people. An intercessor represents the people before God and God before the people. You are the mouth piece of the people that reminds heaven of His promises.

Nehemiah was serving as a cupbearer to the king of Shushan when he received the news that the walls of Jerusalem had been broken and the gates brought down. Walls and gates in Israel were very symbolic. This left the city in a vulnerable state for the enemy to attack God's people. Nehemiah wept over the deplorable state of Jerusalem. The bible, in *Nehemiah 1:4* says:

"And it came to pass, when I heard these words, that I sat down and wept, and mourned certain days, and fasted, and prayed before the God of heaven."

Nehemiah's passion for the people of God moved him to seek the face of God in prayers and fasting. He repented of the sins committed by his fathers and the people of Jerusalem. He recognized that God never steps in to move until we clear the path for Him. Every move of God is preceded by man's genuine repentance.

Favor is for a Purpose

Nehemiah gained favor before the king to go and rebuild the walls and gates of Jerusalem. The king also gave him supplies for the building and endorsed his approval for the journey. The vision of Nehemiah was to restore the glory of Jerusalem and bring the people together again.

His humility before God earned him favor before the king. His intention was godly and pure. His desire was born from a selfless motive; it was for the wellbeing of God's people. God granted him favor and protection because of his pure and sincere intention. God answered his prayers and backed up his actions.

He went at night alone to survey the condition of the land. The Bible says that he didn't disclose his mission to anyone. Hide your dreams. A vision revealed prematurely is exposed to attacks. Keep your mouth closed and survey the land.

But every great vision faces great opposition. Nehemiah's desire to rebuild the walls of Jerusalem was mocked by certain groups but it didn't deter his courage to rebuild the walls of Jerusalem. His intentions were pure before God. He was embarking on a kingdom assignment. That attracted divine favor upon him. You have nothing to fear when you are working in line with God's will for your life.

Know that the vision God gave you will be ridiculed and mocked. The brothers of Joseph mocked his dreams; the brothers of David opposed him; the wife of king David mocked him for dancing recklessly for the Lord in public. Noah was mocked when he was building the giant boat that saved his family. The wife of Job ridiculed him to curse God and die. The mother of Jabez cursed him. Every step of faith always gets attacked. Sometimes attacks from people around you are indications that you've found your calling.

Builders and Warriors

Nehemiah was ready to risk his own life in the process. He fortified the builders, too, in readiness for battle. They were trained to be builders and warriors at the same time. They worked on the broken walls of Jerusalem and watched for the enemy. Nehemiah was not scared of the enemy. He wasn't backing off. He knew God had his back. God sent him on the mission and he had the approval of heaven. No man could stop him.

"Your assignment will infuriate your enemy."

You have the backing of God. No man should scare you. You have a rare commission on earth. Your mandate is divine. Stand up and stand out. Step into your greatness and let the world hear your voice. You are gifted and equipped to change the world. You are not throwing in the towel for any reason. Your vision is worth fighting for. You must be willing to risk your life for your assignment.

The enemy attacked the house of Abraham and took his family members in his absence. Abraham braced up as a leader. He gathered his trained soldiers and strategically went after the enemy and brought back his loved ones. David didn't cry for pity when his city was attacked by the enemy. He received God's approval and went after the enemy. He overtook his enemies and recovered everything lost. God has raised you to take the battle to the gates of the enemy and rescue your generation.

Take your battle to the prayer altar. Fight on your knees. Pray and fast and use God's word to set your home free. You are sent to be an intercessor in that region. Intercessors have incredible compassion for the souls of people. You must be willing to throw your whole life into it. That is how victory is won. Have the courage to keep building and the courage to die if needed.

Rebuilding the Altar

Another trait we can pick from Nehemiah was his life of consecration before God. He didn't only confess his sins and repent before embarking on this mission; he now summoned the people to confess their sins too. The priest led the people into a covenant and oath before the Lord to fear and serve Him. Sin brought about the fall of the wall of Jerusalem. God promised to protect Israel from their enemies and bless them, on the condition that they continue to love Him with all their hearts, their minds and their souls. Sin brings down the walls of divine protection which gives the devil entrance to attack God's people. Covenant is a covering.

The people renewed their oaths before the Lord. They offered sacrifices and dedicated their lives to Him. The rebuilding of the wall was symbolic of their lives being rebuilt by God. The land was cleansed from curse and God's wrath. The fear of God was rekindled in the hearts of the people afresh. The laws were re-enacted in the land. Order precedes every great move of God. Elijah had to rebuild the altar before he called down fire from heaven. God responds to a set atmosphere. Our humility sets the pace for spiritual renewal.

It is wisdom to set spiritual order in our lives and renew our vows before God. Things fall apart when the center crumbles. The covenant is at the center of our relationship with God. The moment one begins to break his vows before the Lord, it gives the devil room to creep in. Heaven responds to order. Restore your consecration and renew your covenant with God.

A Cry for a Reward

Nehemiah showed great selflessness in his work. I observed that it was at end of his assignment that he thought of his reward. He asked God to remember him for good.

Nehemiah 13:14 says:

"Remember me, O my God, concerning this, and wipe not out my good deeds that I have done for the house of my God, and for the offices thereof."

He repeated this same prayer in the last verse in his book, *'remember me, o my God, for good.'* That is the heart of a true intercessor. He sought his reward after he served the people. His personal desire was the very last thing on his agenda. A leader places the needs of the people ahead of his own need. He settles them first and ensures they are safe before he thinks of himself. Your need is not your first priority as a leader. Your followers are your first priority.

God has called you to stand in the gap for your generation. You are the light of hope. Take up the challenge. You are the one they have been waiting for. Take your place and redeem them. You are their savior. You are called to reconcile men back to God.

Nehemiah rose to become a builder and a governor in the land. God honored him because he placed God's kingdom as his first priority. Psalm 91:14-16:

"Because he hath set his love upon me, therefore will I deliver him: I will set him on high, because he hath known my name."

CHAPTER FIVE

RUTH: THE HELPER

"It takes patience to identity the perfect will of God."

Destiny will connect you with the right person. Such connections are not made in consequence of human efforts. God orchestrates it Himself at His time. There are people you meet and it's difficult to turn away from them. Their hearts stay bonded to your soul. There are relationships designed in heaven; like the covenant relationship between David and Jonathan, Mary and Elizabeth, Jesus and John the beloved. Ruth seemed to see something in Naomi that was meant to shape her life. Her desire to cling to her was deeper than the desire to quit. Her resolution was a vow to stick to the end. *Ruth 1:16* says:

"But Ruth said: "Entreat me not to leave you, Or to turn back from following after you; For wherever you go, I will go; And wherever you lodge, I will lodge; Your people shall be my people, And your God, my God."

Ruth showed unwavering faith. She was to embark on a journey to a strange land where she would be considered a stranger. But she was willing to cleave. Her faith in God made her see beyond the deprivation of the present moment into a greater opportunity. Destiny was calling and she had to answer. She was the one chosen to play a major role in history. A story that would produce the greatest king in Israel; a decision that also ushered the King of kings into the world. Ruth would play a part in God's agenda.

The Courage to Cling

Ruth had the guts to turn her back on her own people and go to a people she didn't know, an uncertain mission. She showed a dogged faith. This young widow sacrificed her personal comfort to reach out to a people she never knew. She resolved in her heart to be a part of Naomi's life. Her tenacity to go with Naomi reminds me of Elijah and Elisha. Elisha shut down his business to follow his master to any length. His selfless quest positioned him to receive the mantle of Elijah.

"Faith in God will push you out of your comfort zone."

God chooses people from a place of service. You can trace every divine encounter to a moment of stewardship. God saw the heart of Ruth and found bedrock for His agenda on earth. She was positioned to usher in the greatest man that ever walked the surface of the earth, Jesus Christ. Her selflessness caught the eyes of God. *Ruth 2:2 says:*

"And Ruth the Moabitess said unto Naomi, Let me now go to the field, and glean ears of corn after him in whose sight I shall find grace. And she said unto her, Go, my daughter."

Divine Set Up

Ruth served her way into the field of the wealthiest man in the land. Anything done out of manipulation will not last. Favor cannot be manipulated. You cannot set up the favor of God. David was keeping the sheep and God chose him. Joseph was serving in the prison and God remembered him. The angel of God appeared to Gideon to announce his assignment as he was taking care of his father's business. Stewardship in the kingdom of God is the way to the heart of God. Naomi never told Boaz about Ruth. It wasn't her set up. God was writing the love story Himself.

Encounter with Favor

Boaz took notice of Ruth because of her diligence towards his business. It was not arranged by Naomi. Excellence cannot be hidden. Her tenacity pushed her out to the field to work without pay to take care of Naomi. She volunteered herself.

God picked Ruth. He searched her heart and intentions. The condition of your heart matters. God observes your heart. He never makes mistakes. And He cannot be used or manipulated. He is a perfect and orderly God.

"Then he said, "Blessed are you of the LORD, my daughter! For you have shown more kindness at the end than at the beginning, in that you did not go after young men, whether poor or rich. And now, my daughter, do not fear. I will do for you all that you request, for all the people of my town know that you are a virtuous woman." – Ruth 3:10-11

Humility is the willingness to listen. Ruth followed the counsel of Naomi. Even though God ordained her to be in that field, she still had to listen to the voice of a mentor. Just because you received a divine promise from God is not a proof that it must happen. Yes, I know that sounds strange; but it is very important you understand that God can change His mind on a person. God can reject His chosen one. God's promises can be reversed. His blessings are totally conditional. Salvation is free but blessing has a price tag on it. Consistent obedience is the price to preserve the blessing of God!

Redeemed by Grace

Ruth's godly virtue spoke for her. She had a good testimony because of the decision she made to forsake all and follow God's plan for her life. She knew her uniqueness. She stood out from the crowd. There is something attractive about being different. The wealthiest man in Israel took notice of her. The Bible didn't record it was because of her beauty. Ruth exhibited a godly character. She was diligent, dedicated and committed to her assignment. She didn't seduce Boaz. Her motivation was simply to take care of her mother-in-law who just lost her husband and two sons. Her good intention was observed by many and it got to the ears of Boaz. Ruth served her way into the heart of Boaz.

Those who focus on themselves don't go far in life. But those who focus on being a blessing to others eventually go places. David was alone in the field tending his father's flock and God took notice of him. Joseph was going to visit his brothers to give them some lunch when he was sold out. He kept serving in the master's house, remaining faithful. His master's wife lied against him and he was sent to prison. But he kept serving in the prison. Encouraging everyone and giving them hope. The prison warden took notice of the excellent spirit in him and put him in charge of everything. His leadership was felt in the prison house. He was putting smiles on the faces of the depressed inmates. On recommendation, the king brought him out and handed the entire nation over to him. We collide with destiny at the place of service.

> *"Until the time that his word came to pass,*
> *The word of the LORD tested him.*
> *The king sent and released him,*
> *The ruler of the people let him go free.*
> *He made him lord of his house,*
> *And ruler of all his possessions,*
> *To bind his princes at his pleasure,*
> *And teach his elders wisdom."*
>
> *Psalm 105:19-22*

Daniel was serving the king when other governors ganged up to lie against him. He was sent into the lions' den but God shut the mouth of the lions. He came out and reigned over them all. Even the king bowed down to Daniel to worship him. Daniel was like a god in the land. He reigned by divine wisdom.

You will never go wrong serving. You will never regret following divine instructions. Service in God's kingdom creates a platform for blessings and promotion. Ruth met the wealthiest man in the land because of her selfless service to her mother-law. Honor gives you access to favor. Honor opens doors for you. Honor brings recommendations. You may be skillful or gifted, but I have seen gifted people with weak character. They struggled and died as local champions. Nobody gave a good report about them. Their doors remained shut.

Ruth, a stranger from another land played a vital role in the genealogy of the greatest kings in Israel. David and Solomon came from the loins of Ruth; and Jesus Christ, the King of Kings also came to earth through her generation. Her humility paved way for her. She was chosen on the ground of service. Boaz redeemed her and married her. Great men can identify genuine stewards. But she first came serving and picking after the reapers. Humility does pay off!

"The right decision in life will positively impact the weight of your purpose."

www.ingramcontent.com/pod-product-compliance
Lightning Source LLC
LaVergne TN
LVHW051817080426
835513LV00017B/1995